W9-BEO-030

ROSE-PAINTING
IN NORWAY

RANDI ASKER

ROSE-PAINTING IN NORWAY

DREYER

© Dreyers Forlag A/S
Fred. Olsensgt. 5
Postboks 1153 Sentrum
0153 Oslo 1

ISBN 82-09-10601-5

Printed in Norway 1990
by a.s Joh. Nordahls Trykkeri, Oslo
Translated from the Norwegian
by Ragnar I. Christophersen

W hat is Norwegian rose-painting? Where did it originate, and when did it reach its climax? Is there anything specially Norwegian about it, that distinguishes it from rose-painting in other countries? These and a host of other questions inevitably confront anyone who first makes the acquaintance of this art. In this book, however, only certain salient features, which we hope will throw some lights on some of the above questions, will be dealt with.

What we commonly call rose-painting is essentially a rustic art, far removed from the conventional art of the towns. It is the decorative art of the Norwegian country districts, to be found on the walls, ceilings and furniture of the peasants' houses, as well as on a great number of smaller objects such as ale-bowls, caskets, jugs, and last but not least on all the large wooden clothes chests. Some rose-painters also decorated parish churches.

By rose-painting we mean not only the more or less naturalistic reproduction of roses and other flowers for ornamental purposes, but rustic painting in general with its figure motifs, geometrical patterns and an occasional landscape. The rose-painters were untutored local craftsmen whose only instruction had been at the hands of itinerant artists or older rose-painters, and this explains its fresh and unconventional appeal.

The break-through of Norwegian rose-painting coincides with the great boom enjoyed by rustic art in 18th century Norway, at a time when town and countryside alike were entering on a period of unprecedented prosperity. In many places new agricultural methods and increased sales of timber had given the peasants a certain affluence. With improved communications and trade relations whith the towns urban culture began to exercise a considerable influence on the countryside, in fact, the peasants were no longer members of an isolated community. These new impulses reached the country districts at various times, and were accepted or rejected according to the temper of the people they reached.

It has been humorously suggested that the origin of rose-painting was the peasant's unwillingness to waste time and labour in scouring all the wood-work in his house, but this is hardly true. Painting obviated a certain amount of washing, no doubt, but far more important, it enabled the Norwegian peasant to express his innate love of colour and ornament, of which weaving and «kroting» (chalk-decorations) were earlier expressions.

Perhaps we should first say a few words about the actual peasant interior in the days before rose-painting was a commonplace. The usual dwelling in most parts of East Norway was a so-called «årestue» or hearth-house. This was a dominant type right up to the end of the 17th century, and in some of the remoter mountain valleys it was in use right up to the 19th century. This hearth-house was a dark room, without windows, and with an open fireplace situated in the middle of the hard earth floor. The smoke escaped through an opening in the roof, and walls and inventory were consequently grimed with smoke. The only form of coloured ornament was the woven tapestry which was hung up on festive occasions. In the course of the 17th century great changes were introduced, chief of which was the use of the «peis» or open hearth with a chimney. The «peisestue» or hearth-room had a chimney built in at one corner of the room, wooden floor and windows, and was free from soot. Bright and airy, with its wood-work scoured and dazzling white, it was excellently adapted for ornamentation both in the form of carving and rose-painting.

In the districts of West Norway the smoke-filled «røykstue» – a type of «årestue» – was used as a dwelling-house right up to the year 1800, with one innovation, viz. that the fire-place was moved over to one corner. As it had no chimney, however, the smoke still hung about the room before passing out through the aperture in the roof. This type of dwelling, like the hearth-house, did not invite pictorial decoration, and here too woven tapestries were hung up on special occasions, supplemented later on by «kroting», a sort of chalk-drawing with which the women decorated the dark walls on holidays.

The geometric patterns of this *décor* clearly show its affinity with weaving. Otherwise houses without fire-places were among the first to be painted, both in East and West Norway.

The oldest rural rose-painting in Norway is to be found about the year 1700, and in some districts it survives right up to the year 1850, reaching its peak during the last decades of the 18th and first decades of the 19th century.

The customary decorating of walls and ceiling derives from churches and town houses. There is reason to believe that most of the wealthier merchants had their timbered walls decorated during the Renaissance and Baroque. The

6

latter period, when the Acanthus motif spread its graceful tendrils over walls and ceilings, was unusually rich in *décor*. From the towns, the journeymen painters made their way to the country districts, to paint church interiors, and it was here that the farmer first met the baroque tendril which was to become the great *leitmotiv* of rose-painting.

Decorated inventory and furniture were not unknown in the country. Members of the professional classes, magistrates, etc., transferred to country jobs, introduced ornamented chests, ale-bowls, and tankards. The peasant could also pick up decorated utensils of this nature at fairs. Many of them date from the end of the 16th century and early 17th century, and while some are undoubtedly imports from Germany and Holland, many are the work of artists from Norwegian towns.

The painting on these household articles is thin, transparent almost; the predominating colours are red, yellow, and green, while the ornamentation is that of the Renaissance.

The first ale-bowls painted in the country districts are not very far removed from these early town products, but they are rarely a direct copy, for the rose-painter was not concerned with mere imitation: he developed what he had inherited from past generations, introducing such new ideas as he thought fit. Even if we date the inception of rose-painting to approximately 1700, this does not mean that it is cast in the mould of the current European style. Like all rustic art it is behind the times, though not as outmoded stylistically as we have been given to believe. In style, in fact, rose-painting is a blend of Renaissance, Baroque, Rococo, and Empire, yet bearing all the hallmarks of a tradition which frequently goes right back to the Middle Ages. Current European styles did not always reach the country district at an early stage, while certain stylistic elements are accepted and reproduced according to the fancy of the rose-painter. The result is neither baroque nor rococo, but a lively and charming rustic art *sui generis* – an art which is a gracious blend of new and old. Rose-painting demonstrates admirably the way in which fresh impulses are given different form in different parts of the country, and the local characteristics are so obvious that we can usually tell at a glance where a particular work of art was produced. Form and perhaps even more ornamentation speak to us in the local idiom.

The rose in particular flourishes all over the country, though with varying intensity and in various forms. Certain parts of Norway are essentially rose-painting centres, primarily a continous belt running across South Norway from Østerdalen and the low-lands of the east, via Hallingdal, Numedal, Telemark, Aust-Agder including Setesdal, Vest-Agder, and Rogaland. The west country is comparatively poor in rose-painting, probably because in this part of Norway geometrical motifs were the favourite mode of expression, and these were more suitable for carving than rosepainting. We know little about Møre and North Norway, but in the country of Trøndelag we find a rose-painting centre at Oppdal. Gudbrandsdal is primarily the valley of carving, and here rustic painting made little headway, or was as a rule confined to the painting of carved ornaments.

In the large and flourishing rose-painting districts of South Norway, two localities stand out: Hallingdal and Telemark. Here were a host of local artists, and here rose-painting reached its finest expression. Though we find rose-painting of good quality in other parts of Norway, the actual art of rose-painting is really confined to this part of the country. Artists from Telemark and Hallingdal worked extensively in neighbouring valleys and districts of West-Norway, leaving clear evidence of their work in local painting, and it is from these two districts that impulses spread to other parts of the country. In practically every case rose-painting is intimately related to an interior. At first utensils and furniture – ale-bowls and caskets, cupboards and chests – were painted, and later on the whole room with its bonded walls. In the oldest interiors the acanthus tendril winds its luxuriant growth along the timbers of the room, blue or red on a white ground. This is merely another version of the primitive chalk-painting which was used to decorate the inside of the lids of clothes chests. Later on the walls are painted in oil colours, while the ceiling retains it chalk-paintings. A white ceiling made the room appear larger and brighter. Gradually the tenrils were drawn in larger patterns covering several beams (cf. pages 17, 18 and 26). Various scenes, embodying figures, are framed in rococo patterns, or in a Louis-Seize or Empire frame. The wall behind the high-seat is first panelled, and this panel requires its own special *décor*, which is distinct from the rest of the wall. The same special attention is given to the panel behind the bed. These panels are frequently decorated with figure motifs, possibly a relic of the old wall tapestries. *The Wise and Foolish Virgins*, for example, a popular motif in the tapestries of the 17th century, occasionally re-appear, this time as paintings. Other scenes are taken from illustrated Bibles and pamphlets, or we have royal personages and military leaders, as well as religious scenes and strange animals. Popular scenes, however, are always taken from the world as it exists in the mind of the rose-painter, and we find the example on a door in Telemark a picture of the local fiddler (cf. page 19). In the same room we frequently find native and exotic ornamentation and figures side by side.

It is in the ornamentation, in the actual roses, that the rural touch is most obvious. The *leitmotiv* of rose-painting is the baroque tendril. This is perhaps most apparent in Hallingdal and Telemark, where it predominates in the first half of the 18th century, while its subsequent development differs widely in these two districts. Undoubtedly the elegant motifs of the baroque tendril appeal strongly to the Hallingdal peasant. This was something which suited his temperament, something that he understood and found easy to reproduce.

The oldest rose painter known to us from Hallingdal is Truge Gunhildgard from Ål (born approx. 1690, died some time in the 1760's). He has decorated several rooms in the old technique, using chalks. His most characteristic feature is an oldfashioned and vigorous tendril, set off with bird and animal figures. Better known – and a more significant artist – than Gunhildgard is Kittil Rygg from Hol (born approx. 1727, died 1809), the founder of the Hallingdal school. As early as 1759, in the Nestgardstuen, he paints his baroque tendril boldly and unerringly, with little use of contour and with a broad and sweeping brush. But he also paints the old heroes of the chronicles, King Karl and King Holger the Dane (cf. page 41). These figures are undoubtedly based on early models, but on the chest-ends Kittil Rygg's own tendril predominates. In these chests reposed the farmer's dearest possessions the family's clothes and jewels – and it is not surprising that they were beautifully painted and richly mounted. They were passed down from generation to generation and regarded as precious heirlooms.

As far as we know, Kittil Rygg had no direct followers, but his younger contemporary Kristen Aanstad (born 1746, died 1832) had clearly learned a lot form him. Aanstad moved to Hallingdal from Gudbrandsdal, and his rose-painting reveals, not so much in the roses as in the colour, that he was not a genuine native of Hallingdal. When painting chests and cupboards he generally used a blue or green ground, while a red ground was used almost exclusively in Hallingdal. He had adapted a rococo C shape, using it in a tendril – generally blue or white in colour – interrupted by rosettes. The feature of his art is that it erupts beyond the boundaries of the picture surface, sending a shower of roses across the figured wall and frame (cf. page 34). But we forgive him his extravagance in view of the life and gaiety he creates. In some of his works, moreover, he proves that he can confine himself to a limited area (cf. pages 42 and 43).

Herbrand Sata (born 1753, died 1830), a Hallingdal rococo artist, was a greater master than Kristen Aanstad. The rococo cartouches of is earlier work from the 1780's suggest that he has had some contacts with urban art. But in his mature style, which we have every right to call true Halling painting, we find a great deal of floral Baroque (cf. pages 35 and 42). When he decorates a chest, he makes each of the two halves of its *facade* an artistic entity in itself, one harmonizing effectively with the other (cf. page 42). Each half has a central point: a flower or an animal, surrounded by a frame of flowers, rhythmically composed of roses and tulips. The contours are not outstanding, for the Hallingdal artist is principally concerned with colour, achieving his effect by contrasting one colour with another, especially bright clear colours. Here we have blue or green mountings against a cinnabar background. Herbrand Sata frequently uses a red background colour for the roses, marking off the petals in blue or white, with touches of yellow and green. In his colourful interiors the walls are usually painted in oils and the ceiling is still usually decorated with red and blue tendrils, done in chalk. He has a firm and graceful stroke, and a real mastery of figure motifs not to be found in his predecessors. His work covers the entire development from baroque and rococo to the characteristic Hallingdal painting. Kittil Rygg adopted the acanthus tendril, but Herbrand Sata introduces floral baroque seen through the eyes of a Hallingdal man.

Among all his pupils we remember principally his two sons Embrik, (born 1788, died 1876) and Niels Bæra (born 1785, died 1873), who continue and develop the Hallingdal style. Niels Bæra is the more important. In his interiours (cf. page 36) he retains his father's love of contrast, using red and blue-green on walls and inventory, while his ceilings have the characteristic bright chalk-painting with a luxuriant rococo ornamentation in the red and blue. A ceiling decoration such as we see on page 36 shows that already in one of his first works his style underwent a change from his Father's acanthus tendril to rococo. The religious scenes portrayed on the walls are given elegant rococo frames. An innovation is that they tend to stand out from their background and that he starts to work with perspective. Tastefully and unerringly he decorated chests and cupboards with roses, which for all time have remained a typical example of the Halling rose.

Niels Bæra was a school-teacher, a profession which gave him an unusually fine and firm handwriting. He had many pupils, both directly and indirectly, one of the most skilled of whom was Paal Grøt (born 1812, died 1906). He frequently uses a black ground, on which he puts deep cinnabar and lush green as contrasts. In the smaller roses he adds a touch of gold. Paal Grøt uses Niels Bæra's acanthus, not as a tendril, but as a single leaf (cf. page 47), and he also shows a penchant for exotic animals, which he paints very effectively on a white ground crowned by red and green leaves. Paal Grøt himself is a skilled artist, though rather limited in range, and he probably made several of the chests and cupboards which he decorated.

Another of Niels Bæra's pupils, Torstein Sand from Hol (born 1808, died 1887), paints in a style highly reminiscent of Paal Grøt's. Far more productive than the latter, he worked in his later years for the most part in Uvdal in Numedal, painting several notable interiors in a style that set new local standards.

While rose-painters from Ål and Hol were very active in Lower Hallingdal, it would be wrong not to mention a number of local artists, such as Sjugurd Sørbel of Gol (born 1827, died 1901) and Engebret Rime of Flå (born approx. 1808, died 1884). Both were active in the 1840's, and their work bears evidence of contract with the Telemark school. In fact both Upper and Lower Hallingdal at this period reflect to some extent the influence of Telemark, an influence that was even more marked in the 1850's. There is noe doubt that this impulse came from artists of an entirely different temperament.

In its more developed form Telemark painting has borrowed from the rococo, but this rustic art, too, derives from a wholesome virile baroque tendril. One of the first to take up this motif in the rustic painting of Telemark was a certain Talleiv Maalar. The town influence here is obvious, and it becomes even more striking when he works with running acanthus motifs, as in an interiour from Rauland in Telemark. The curved garland of the *Régence* is otherwise only infrequently represented in peasant art, in painting or carving. In the middle of this urban acanthus décor he has placed a country bridal procession.

A clear example of the relation between town and country-painting is also found in the work of the well-known painter and wood-carver. Thomas Blix (born ca. 1677), who painted tendril décor in a few Telemark churches in 1713 and 1714 (cf. pages 17 and 18). At the same time he painted ale-bowls for some of the farms situated nearest these churches. As a rule he decorated the bowls with pictures of the princes participating in the great Nordic War, or their capitals, framed in acanthus tendrils. These bowls have actually become the prototype for bowls painted in Telemark, while his characteristic tendril style re-appears in the work of several later rose-painters.

Telemark, however, is not a large cohesive district like the great valley of Hallingdal. In its numerous little valleys and remote communities a great many local schools of painting grew up: in fact, we know the names of over a hundred Telemark rose-painters. One of the earliest and most outstanding was Olav Hansson (born 1750, died 1820) who painted several interiors between 1780 and a little after 1800. The white-washed walls provide a bright and cosy atmosphere and form an exellent background to his red or green cupboards and doors (cf. pages 17, 19 and 26). Olav Hansson has a special fondness for the animals of the fables, as well as popular folk motifs of various kinds, but he is at his best in the roses. He excels at at good powerful baroque tendril, occasionally in combination with the familiar roses of floral baroque or certain rococomotifs. In a few interiors he uses the curved garland and tendrils of the Régence style to frame the picture surface (cf. page 17). He bases his *décor* both on the baroque tendril, Régence, and rococo shell ornamentation, fusing these elements in a picturesque monumental style. He has a broad elegant brush, with the clear contour drawing of the Telemark painter.

Olav Hansson had a great number of successors in East Telemark. But while he and many of his school were mostly influenced by baroque tendril painting, the painters of West Telemark were more prone to affect a rococo style, and several artists here – especially in the Vinje and Rauland districts – were also figure painters. Their work was hardly academic, but the richly decorated frames usually gave their interiours an air of unusual gaiety. Aslak Nestestog (born 1758, died 1830), one of the earliest of these painters, had also decorated church interiors. Bjørn Bjaalid (born 1791, died 1862) (cf. page 29) is gay and entertaining while the somewhat younger Halvor Asbjørnson Teigen (born 1818, died 1909) has a firmer sense of line (cf. page 33).

Both Åmotsdal and Kviteseid had their school of painting, often markedly rococo, as the fine chest reproduced on page 28, the work of an unknown master, shows. Olaf Torjusson (born 1754, died 1828), who founded a school in Åmotsdal, painted a number of interiors (cf. page 20). Of the better known Seljord and Kviteseid artists we should mention Olav Guttormson Langerud (born 1782, died 1844), who also founded a school, and Knut Mevasstaul (born 1785, died 1862).

From Fyresdal we have a magnificent painter, Nikuls Buine (born 1789, died 1852), who was responsible for the richly and elegantly painted chest shown on page 27. In the Heddal–Hjartdal district the best known painter was Hans Glittenberg (born 1788, died 1873). He decorated a great many domestic interiors, and had a number of pupils, as did also Thomas Luraas (born 1799, died 1886), who partly influenced the Glittenberg School. The Luraas family, which produced so many master-fiddlers and rose-painters, had its home in Tinn, where rose-painting got going rather later than elsewhere, but subsequently reached great heights.

The name of Thomas Luraas is known far beyond the boundaries of his native Telemark. He probably travelled around more than most rose-painters. He visited Hallingdal and Numedal a couple of times, and ranged about West Norway from Romsdal to Rogaland, leaving behind him everywhere traces of his influence. With his two brothers he founded a school of painters. He has painted a great many farmhouse interiors, evincing a weakness for generals and royal personages in uniform (cf. pages 24 and 31) undoubtedly taken from models, though most of them have a characteristic Telemark frame-work.

The typical Telemark rose, of which Luraas is a master, has been compared to a plant with roots, stem, leaves, and flowers (cf. pages 21 and 30). A rococo C forms the stem, a smaller c placed sideways represents the roots, and the flowers are perched on slender stems in group of three. This rose can be adapted to practically any field, constituting the principal motif, and is never framed, as in the Hallingdal style, where there is a symmetrical, composition about a central point. Sometimes the Telemark rose is long and slender, at others more concentrated and rounded. In the hands of the rose-painters it acquires endless variety, but a common feature in every case is the C-shaped principal motif and above all a marked contour drawing in black or white. The slender elegant contours are drawn with an incredibly fine brush, made of a few hairs from the tail of a squirrel. A feature of the Telemark painter's art is his insistence on draughtsmanship, on the actual line of the ornament and all the small details (cf. page 24). The Telemark rose is the fruit of temperaments which differs materially from the bold rose-painting of Hallingdal. Characteristic of the rose-painters of Telemark, as well as Hallingdal and several other districts, is that many of them were expert fiddlers.

Numedal, midway between Telemark and Hallingdal, has received impulses from both these rose-painting strongholds, first from Hallingdal in the north and later from Telemark further south. Several versions of the Telemark rose, and a marked style of contour drawing, suggest that the Telemark influence was the strongest. A few of the Numedal artists, however, manage to create their own style. The oldest of these was Thore Kravig from Nore (b. 1748, d. 1810); basing himself on the c-shapes of rococo he develops a highly characteristic tendril which provides the principal motif in a Flesberg interior from 1776. As a rule he decorates chests (page 50) with roses of red, white and blue against a black background. Kittil Haukjem from Veggli (b. 1774, d. 1859) is esssentially a rococo artist with a brush that combines sureness of touch and great lightness; he composes his roses with an unerring eye to the panels to be covered (p. 54) and is notable for the elegance of his outlines. Haukjem has decorated several rooms, often introducing a fine and varied marbling. Another outstanding Numedal master was Sebjørn Kverndalen (born 1786, died 1875), who learnt his art at Kongsberg, where he probably made the acquaintance of «chinoiserie» (cf. page 38). The peacock seems to have been his favourite motif, and it might almost be said to have been his signature. He was an elegant and highly trained artist, maintaining a high standard right up to his last years. Kverndalen is also believed to have painted in Sigdal, where the same outside influences were felt as in Numedal.

Gudbrand Larsen Foss (b. 1759, d. 1844) from Sigdal was a competent and very exuberant rococo painter, a pastmaster at decorating. He is responsible for embellishing numerous travelling chests with his characteristic roses (p. 55). A cupboard from 1792 (c.p. 52) reveals his lively tulips painted in red on a white ground. The somewhat younger Gunnar Målarn, or Veggesrudlia, as he was called (b. 1798, d. 1869), composed a number of interiors and decorated countless chests.

Not much painting has come down to us from the coastal strip of the county of Aust-Agder in South Norway. A number of Telemark painters, as well as some from the neighbouring county of Vest-Agder, made their way here. But Aust-Agder has bred an outstanding rococo painter in Salve Torjusson Flaten. He paints the tendril with playful ease and gives the rococo motifs a completely personal form. In Setesdal, which was virtually cut off from intercourse with the outside world, medieval forms remained longer than elsewhere in the country. Rose-painting makes a belated entry, and though there were a great many rose-painters, they found it difficult to compete on equal terms with the artists of Telemark and Vest-Agder who came to Setesdal. We should, however, mention the name of Valle Degn, who

14

painted a number of ale-bowls and chests in the middle of the 18th century.

The close contact which the coastal districts enjoyed with Holland and North Germany favoured the growth of floral baroque in this part of Norway. In the county of Vest-Agder there is hardly any rococo influence; instead the tendril and floral baroque predominate. Here, too, rose-painting comes late, not becoming general until about 1780, though lasting for a hundred years. Best known of the rose-painters is Thore Risøyne (born 1762), who painted Grindheim Church in 1783 (cf. page 49). Later comes Olav Kvinlaug (born 1773), who is believed to have decorated the Mjåland «loft» in 1800 (cf. page 40). The Vest-Agder specialist in this style, Guttorm Persson Eftestøl, founded a local school. A feature of this district is the deep blue or dark ground, sometimes with white decorated fields, which reminds us of the dark hues of the local tapestries.

Rogaland was visited by artists both from Hallingdal and Telemark, and consequently we get one district showing Hallingdal influence, one with a Telemark influence, and one district with a good native type of rose-painting. In West Norway we find a few descendants of the Telemark rose, frequently on a red ground, possibly a reminder of the Hallingdal influence. A red background is also used by the artists of Hardanger, the western centre of rose-painting.

So far little research has been done on the art of North Norway, and our knowledge of painting in Trøndelag is also incomplete. It seems that the painters here found it difficult to break away from the Renaissance ornamentation of the town-inspired painted ale-bowls. They tend to use few and dark colours, and their acanthus seems dry and stylised. As a contrast we have the Vikastue from Oppdal, painted in 1795, one of the finest rococo works of our native art (cf. page 53), traditionally ascribed to Knut Honne. The ceiling panels between the rafters are decorated with a rather broad-leaved rococo tendril, whose contours are in every way equal to the best Telemark work.

In other respects painting in Oppdal and to some extent in the Møre district seems to have been inspired by the work of the Gudbrandsdal craftsmen Peder Kristensen Selsjord – or Målar Per as he was called – from Lesja, who settled in Aure in Nord-Møre, exerting no little influence on painting locally.

In the Gudbrandsdal rose-painting played a somewhat modest role compared to wood-carving, but a number of painters are known to us. Their motifs show the same acanthus as in wood-carving, until the town-bred painter Peder Veggum starts decorating cupboards and cabinets with his town-inspired figure scenes. In a class by himself we have the characteristic wood-carver and painter Kristen Listad, an example of whose rich and varied rococo work is to be found on a trousseau chest he decorated for his own daughter (cf. page 40).

In the rose-painting of East Norway's lowlands floral baroque undoubtedly played the most important role. One of the most famous master painters was Peder Aadnes (born 1739, died 1792) (cf. page 46), who really bridges the gap between town and country. He painted portraits, cupboards, and chests, as well as landscapes on wall-panels, in a number of country districts. He has a rich luxuriant style, a delicate brush and a cultured palette.

One of his many imitators was Ole Hermundsen Berge from Sør-Aurdal in Valdres (b. 1768, d. 1826). Among other things he decorated the interiors of churches in Nord-Aurdal and Vestre Slidre, borrowing Aadnes's floral motifs and colours. Both colours and motifs on the cupboard shown on page 48 are typical of this master.

The Sjøli painters in Sør-Østerdal were also influenced by Aadnes and by the landscape painting that was being executed in the lowlands of East Norway. The most important of them is Ole Halstensen Sjøli (d. 1827), who is believed to have learned his craft from Peder Aadnes. He painted several rococo interiors, among them the room at Hovslykkja at Hernes, (p. 50), generally using white and blue as his chief colours. In his later work there are clear traces of classical influence.

In the second half of the last century rose-painting had reached the end of its tether, after flourishing for close on 150 years. «Oak-grain painting» and painting in white became the rage in the country, destroying the old sense of colour.

If we are to select certain features of our rose-painting, which distinguish it from that of other countries, we must remember Norway's somewhat remote geographical position as well as the difficult internal communications, which placed great emphasis on tradition. New ideas were absorbed slowly, not merely because the peasant was conservative, but equally because he had a distinct sense of style and a very decided attitude to his art. The process of adaptation which occurs in every valley makes Norwegian rose-painting more varied than abroad, and in conclusion we may suggest that there is a peculiarly Norwegian sense of colour characterised by a love of pure bright hues, which tends to produce and effect of vivid contrast.

Above: The so-called "oppstue", in Telemark, was beautifully decorated. This interior, from Mellem-Ryen, Heddal, was painted by Olav Hansson in 1782. The back of the "High Seat" has a picture showing the Baptism of Our Lord, while the ceiling has scenes from the Crucifixion, entwined between tendrils, as well as the Dragon and the seven-headed monster. Below: Panel from Kviteseid Church, Telemark, painted in 1714 by the town painter and wood-carver Thomas Blix.

Tendril décor painted straight onto the timbered wall of a room at Suigard Midgarden, Rauland, Telemark, the work of Talleiv Maalar, one of the earliest rose-painters known to us from Telemark.

The townpainter Thomas Blix painted a few churches in Telemark, and at the same time decorated a number of ale bowls in the nearby farms. The one shown is dated 1713, and comes from Tveito in Vinje.

The fiddler was one of the most important members of a rural community in olden times. Here he appears on a door in Heddal, Telemark. The painting is the work of Olav Hansson.

Above: Painted interior from about 1750 from Torvetjønn in Rauland. Below: Olav Torjusson who founded a school in Aamotsdal, painted this rococo-like interior at Djuve in Øyfjell, Telemark.

Combined bed and cupboard, of a type frequently found locally, at Nedre Lynnevik, Gransherad, Telemark. Typical Telemark roses painted in 1838 by Knut Halvorsen Hovde.

Detail of a fine chest from Vindlaus farm, Eidsborg in Telemark, painted about 1800.

Typical Telemark chest from Solberg in Drangedal. Solidly bound with metal, the chest has a fine rose décor, painted in 1810 by a craftsman with a sure and well schooled hand.

Room at Norigard Berdal farm in Vinje, Telemark, decorated with several figure panels. Between the windows can be seen the prophets Jeremiah and Daniel, painted in 1821 by Sveinung Svalastog.

Above: Part of the ceiling at Gunvaldjord, Haukeli, Telemark, painted by Thomas Luraas in 1840. The roses are to a certain extent combined with the Régence «broken band».

Below: The purely ornamental tends to predominate in the work of the rural painters. Door panel from Telemark. Tjukan Museum.

Door panels were often decorated in a way which was admirably adapted to their size. This one from Donstad in Morgedal, Telemark, was painted in 1850 by Knut Mevasstaul from Seljord.

Several of the West Telemark painters tried their hand at figure painting. These two cupboard doors, made in 1787 at Norigard Hylland, Vinje, Telemark, were the work of Aslak Nestestog.

Interior and ceiling decoration from Ramberg, Heddal, Telemark, painted by one of the older Telemark rose-painters, Olav Hansson, in 1781. The ceiling is done in chalk, the dresser and bed in oils.

26

Nikuls Buine, Fyresdal, was an elegant painter, as this detail from a chest from Brunkeberg shows. Painted 1833.

Side of a chest, with an unusually light background colour and exquisite contours. This markedly rococo chest is from Kviteseid in Telemark, painted in 1782 by an unknown artist.

Bjørn Bjaalid's decorations frequently contain figures in an elegant floral frame. This cupboard from Øvre Mo in Rauland, Telemark, was painted in 1828.

Typical Telemark rose with root, stem, leaves and flowers, and line drawing in black and white. Door panel from Telemark painted by one of Olav Guttormsen's pupils. Property of Kai Fjell, Oslo.

Thomas Luraas had a predilection for kings, generals and other persons in uniform. This knight appears on a door panel at Hvalen farm in Tinn, Telemark, painted about 1850.

Both the brushwork and the lines of rose painting bear closer inspection, as is shown in this detail of a chest from Telemark, painted in 1869 by Halvor Jonsjord.

Detail of a chest painted in Rauland by Halvor Asbjørnson Teigen in 1848. Large and small roses are interwined, though not with the unerring touch of the older painters.

Above: Kristen Aanstad was both joiner and painter. On the first floor of the Ruiloft at Hol, Hallingdal, we find him as a rose painter, where his blue and white rococo painting covers panels and mouldings. The sea-horse on the door, painted in 1776, was a favourite motif.

Below: Herbrand Sata's earliest work was not very far removed from the rococo painting of the towns. Chest from Aal, Hallingdal, painted in 1789. Drammens Museum, Drammen.

Above: Embrik Bæra, son of Herbrand Sata, was given his first major commission as a painter in 1824, decorating Villandsstuen at Hol (now in the Hallingdal Folk Museum). Detail of gable panel with a mounted warrior.

Below: A decorative panel with a lion on a halberd surrounded by foliage; part of a panel from Torpo, Hallingdal, now in Drammens Museum. Painted by Herbrand Sata c. 1800.

The walls of Hallingdal farms were often painted in oils, while the ceiling was done in white chalk with red and blue tendrils. Interior from Myking in Aal, painted by Niels Bæra in 1827. Norwegian Folk Museum.

By the 1830's the Hallingdal painters had already evolved their own special style. Cupboard from Aal, painted by Niels Bæra in 1838. Norwegian Folk Museum.

Above: Chinoiserie was late in reaching the rustic artists of Numedal. Chest from Flesberg, painted in 1800.
Below: The peacock appears so frequently in the work of Sebjørn Kverndalen from Nore that it might almost be regarded as his signature. Cupboard décor from Uvdal Numedal. Both in Norwegian Folk Museum.

Hallingdal mug with spout, from Aal, painted in 1841. Property of the Norwegian Folk Museum. This type of mug was both decorative and functional. On festive occasions ale was poured from it into ale bowls, which were passed round the table. Silver and porcelain versions also existed.

Above: Interior from the Mjaalandsloft, Vest-Agder, painted by Olav Kvinlaug in 1800.
Below: Magnificent trousseau chest painted by Kristen Listad of Gudbrandsdal for his
daughter in 1784.

The Chronicle heroes
King Karl and Holger
the Dane were often
carved on powder horns
as early as the 17th cen-
tury. "King Olger the
Dane" – detail of a chest
from Hol, Hallingdal,
now in the Norwegian
Folk Museum. The out-
side was painted in oils
in the 1780's by Kittel
Rygg, while the chalk
painting inside is pre-
sumably of earlier date.

Thomas Luraas from
Tinn was not the only
painter with a penchant
for depicting military figures. Detail of a clock
from Sigdal, painted by
Sebjørn   Kverndalen
from Nore, Numedal.
Norwegian Folk Mu-
seum.

Above: Typical Halling chest. Red ground, a central point with a framework of flowers and a minimum of contour line. This chest from Aal was painted by Herbrand Sata. Norwegian Folk Museum.

A woodcut of one of the Danish kings probably served as a model for this illustration to the above painting by Kristen Aanstad. From Aal in Hallingdal, now in the Drammens Museum.

Chest from Aal, Hallingdal, painted on the outside in typical Hallingdal style by Niels Bæra in 1848. The vigorous baroque tendril on the inside is of earlier date. Norwegian Folk Museum.

The flower-pot was a favourite motif, though this colour combination was rarely found in Hallingdal. Detail of wall cupboard from Aal, Hallingdal, now in the Drammens Museum.

The lion and the unicorn often occurred side by side on decorated chests. The above, from Hallingdal, painted in 1799, belongs to Herbrand Sata's best works.

Peder Aadnes from South Land travelled around the country, decorating interiors and painting portraits, cupboards and chests. His tulips and roses set the fashion for such ornamentation in a number of East Norwegian lowland districts. Chest of drawers from East Gausdal, Gudbrandsdal, painted by Peder Aadnes. Norwegian Folk Museum.

Detail of the cupboard shown on page 51. Paal Grøt often places his exotic animals effectively against a lighter background, and makes good use of the complementary colours.

48

Above: Interior from Grindheim Church, Vest-Agder, painted in 1783 by rose-painter Tore Risøyne from Fjotland. The basic colour is white. Below: Detail from the interior shown above.

Cupboard painted in 1797 by
Ole Hermundsen Berge
of Valdres. Property of the
Norwegian Folk Museum.

Chest from Flesberg, Numedal, painted by Thore Kravig of Nore in 1793. Property of Drammens Museum.

Detail of cupboard panel from Hovslykkja Farm, Hernes. Painted by Ole Halstensen Sjøli, probably some time in the 1770's. Property of the Glomdal Museum.

Paal Grøt, one of Niels Bæra's aptest pupils, is rather bolder in his colour contrast than his
master. Wall cupboard from Aal, Hallingdal, painted in 1833. Norwegian Folk Museum.

Dresser from Sigdal with characteristic tulip ornamentation. Painted by Gudrand Larsen Foss in 1792. Property of Drammens Museum.

Detail of ceiling from Vikastuen in Oppdal. Property of the Trondheim and Trøndelag Folk Museum. Painted in 1795, probably by Knut Honne.

Cupboard door from Øvre Sandsvær, painted in 1806 by the rococo master Kittil Haukjem from Veggli. Property of Drammens Museum.

54

Travelling chest from Sigdal, painted by Gudbrand Larsen Foss in 1782 for his brother Eiliv Larsen Foss. Property of Drammens Museum.